Sexual Techniques

Sexual Techniques

An Illustrated Guide

Text: MOGENS TOFT

Photos: JOHN FOWLIE

SOUVENIR PRESS

© SV PRESS A/S, Copenhagen, 1968
Tegninger af Mie Luf
Translation © copyright 1969 Souvenir Press
All rights reserved

First British edition published September 1969
by Souvenir Press Ltd., 43 Great Russell Street
London, WC1B 3PA

Printed in Great Britain by
Redwood Burn Limited, Trowbridge

Reprinted September 1969
Reprinted October 1969
Reprinted February 1970
Reprinted August 1970
Reprinted December 1970
Reprinted May 1971
Reprinted August 1971
Reprinted August 1972
Reprinted July 1973
Reprinted March 1974
Reprinted December 1974
Reprinted January 1980
Reprinted July 1981

ISBN 0 285 50267 0

CONTENTS

Preface 7

Variation in Sexual Intercourse 12

Anatomy of Sexual Intercourse 14

Positions 25

The Sexual Organs 112

The Functions 113

Sexual Reactions 114

The Male Sex Organs 116

The Female Sex Organs 121

The Vagina 126

The Labia 129

The Clitoris 131

The Female Orgasm 133

Sex and Pregnancy 137

PREFACE

This is a clean and clear book. There is no obscenity; no pornography and the book is all about education.

The unwholesome moralistics in sex education are promoted by the ambivalence of our attitude to sex. On one hand we have reached great permissiveness, and more and more young people, married and unmarried, are experimenting with sex. They feel that sex is part of a life-regulating rhythm in their makeup and the urgent pressure for fulfillment is not repressed or resisted; nor is the Freudian advocacy for sublimation taken overly serious by the young. In fact whatever the merits or demerits of the Kinsey Reports may have been, his deflation of sublimation has made a lasting impression and remain a valid contribution to sexology.

However, the sexual behaviour patterns of society, which are continued from generation to generation, are still active and sexual prudery, anxiety and fear are still present. There are millions of young and young middle-aged people whose basic attitude to sex seems frozen in a Victorian fashion.

Sex education was, and still is, the real victim of this muddle. It is literally the hot potato nobody will handle; the hot chestnut nobody is going to haul out of the fire. Children are still brought up in total ignorance of sexual love and sexual life. Sex organs are still treated like forbidden fruits and the way parents teach their children or teacher teaches pupil or professor teaches students, is to all intents and purposes non-existent.

When suddenly a young man and woman meet, then blissful ignorance which would be unbearable and intolerable in every other faculty of life, is being accepted in the sexual field, in fact, there is a high price and praise for it. Having had sexual knowledge, training and experience would certainly "devalue" the female partner as "soiled ware."

It is still presumed that no education is needed, no learning, no subsequent teaching and understanding, but that perfection falls on the players like a gift from the heavens.

For once we get teaching where we need it most. We get our teaching in word and picture, in diagrams and photographs. The teaching is about sex and the sexual life of man and woman because, as we said above, what the layman knows about it, so far, is likely to fit the back of a postage stamp, and often even the professional shows fixed prejudices rather than knowledge.

When people live in ignorance they develop their own mythologies. If you sit in the psychiatrist's chair or listen, as a general practioner, to the sexual mythology of your patients, of both sexes and all ages, the myths of all early prehistoric happenings are peanuts in comparison to the fables people present.

There are fables about the sex organs, their topography their construction, and their function. There are, for example, mythological ways to spend hours and hours in active sexual combat which puts Casanova and other famous lovers out of business.

There are fantastic ideas about fertility and infertility. Young people taking unprotected risk, trusting in moonphases, in safe periods and in their own sterility. The projection of illness onto sex-organs and functions are prodigious.

I could continue this catalogue of mythological manifestations and absurdum but unfortunately the one aspect of living together, which is not mythological, is very often forgotten: that is the happy knowledge of one's sexual prowess in the pursuit of happiness and in the prevention of the breakup of one's love life.

This unfortunately is the other side of the moon. Where there is lack of knowledge, where there is ignorance, boredom creeps into the human relationship and once the honeymoon is over, there is a flattening of the relationship which often precedes the later breakup. The colossal rate of divorce and the even greater rate of marital unhappiness stands witness for our lack of sex-education.

The approach of this book is very valuable because it combines great easiness of presenting the very complex material with a beautiful way of showing the basic positions of lovemaking which are like the sculptures of a Michelangelo or, in a more modern way, the Norwegian sculpture of Vigeland. It also has a clarity of vision of the great painters like Edward Munch. The fulfilment of the love-potential of two human beings, when freed from pornographic snigger or from the expected stimulation of the frustrated, is rightly being practiced by all civilizations, bar our own, and the author of the book is quoting the big sources of oriental erotic literature like the *Arabian Nights, Kama-Sutra* and the *Perfumed Garden,* and we can add the *Ars Amandi* of the Romans, which is still readable, as examples: so is the sexual history of the Jews which has recently been described by Allen Edwardes in his book *Erotica Judica,* (Julian Press, 1967).

Our major concern to introduce this book is to present another dimension and another aspect of sexual happiness of man and woman, that is: the deepening of their affection, the deepening of their emotional involvement with each other to an extent so that their love-life becomes the heartpiece of their living. When this position of integration of sex-knowledge has been reached, a major step in the health of the people of the world will be foreseeable.

The very humane and reasonable deflation of the idea of the overwhelming importance of the vaginal orgasm instead of acceptance of reaching a clitoridal orgasm, in fact, any orgasm, irrespective of what part of the anatomy is being the agent to promote the sensory intake, makes this become a formidable scientific contribution.

The sexological theories of Freud and Reich, have all been built on the presumption that there is a normal functioning person on the physiological and psychological level and that the neurotically or psychotically ill person is a special case based on a special traumatic constellation, and this against a background of a normal, healthy society.
Reich modified this and accepted the formation of a character neurosis as socially conditioned by a sick society, which must mean, de facto, in all of us, but he too thought that, for instance, the physiological vaginal orgasm and the orgasm reflex can be recalled on

a totally uninhibited depth in everybody and, in fact, in his writings, mainly in *The Function of the Orgasm*, the major goal of Reichian therapy is the rehabilitation of the "normal orgasm reflex".

With the special education as given in this book, the chances that real fridigity in the woman can be over-come as part of it is of unique educative value.

The suffering of frustrated women for whom doctors and psychiatrists set an unreachable goal such as the vaginal orgasm, will be helped by this book and one hopes that they will find greater peace in self-acceptance of reaching a happy climax somehow.

I am very proud to be able to introduce this book to the British public. I feel that the happiness it may give to thousands and thousands of young people by increasing their knowledge and making their sex life happier is a positive and progressive contribution to our living.

Robert Ollendorff
M.A., M.D., L.R.C.P., M.R.C.S., D.P.M.

*W. Reich, Orgone Press 1942, New York

The Various Positions of sexual intercourse

The ways in which coition can be varied are endless. A married couple, Jerome and Julia Rainer, mentioned 206 positions (in their book *Variety and Change in Sexual Life*) which it was claimed could lead to orgasm for both partners. Other authors think that sexual intercourse in 64, 289, or even over 600 positions is possible. The classical oriental textbooks on the art of love-making describe a large number of positions, some of which demand the application of complicated technical tricks such as using pulleys fixed to the ceiling (the position which in a certain American translation of the *Kama Sutra* has acquired the engaging name "Banana Split") and numerous other technical refinements.

However, reading through the literature on the subject of love one finds a good deal of repetition in the repertoire. This is not necessarily to be ascribed to the fact that the number of possible positions is in fact limited: the reason is simply that the ways of describing them were gradually used up.

For those having sexual intercourse it often happens that even quite a small movement of some part of the body or a change in its balance can produce an erotic effect which for *them* means so much that one can speak of a new position. But for the author, no matter whether he is writing with slate, feather or typewriter, the only things which can be treated as new, theoretical details are those which are so difficult to describe that they stand apart from the endless number of other ways of having intercourse.

This book is thus not intended as a step-by-step instruction manual, which is what they often are when accompanying complicated and exotic forms of sexual intercourse. Its purpose is to give guidance, in simple language, so that any couple who are sexually experienced in their relationships with each other can bring variety and change into their life together.

Cohabitation has many sides to it and sex is only one of them; but on the other hand it is the one which directly or indirectly has the greatest influence upon our whole existence. If the sexual side of life is made boring by routine this can become a threat to other aspects of life.

As already stated, the list of sexual positions shown in this book is not exhaustive. The number of variations is endless; but as far as most people are concerned the point to notice is that they are based on fundamental positions which are really very few in number. It is these which we describe here, together with a selection of those which can be easily adapted from the basic positions. And these ought to give adequate inducement towards innumerable experiments — successful ones, we trust.

The Anatomy of Sexual Intercourse

All the positions can really be regarded as modifications or developments of the fundamental ones. The well-known American expert on sex, R. L. Dickinson, maintains (in his "Atlas of Sex Anatomy" pub. 1949) that it is really only a matter of two basic positions, with variations based on these. Dickinson classifies the positions in the following two categories: a) Coition in a prone or semi-supine position: b) sexual intercourse in a more or less upright position. While this is correct from an anatomical point of view it seems to be a gross over-simplication in actual practice. The choice of the 42 positions treated here is based on the following four categories which all have certain features in common:

a) The woman lies on her back, with the man over her.

b) The woman lies on her stomach on the man.

c) Positions in which the introduction of the penis is from the back.

d) Positions in which the insertion of the penis is from the front, the man and woman standing or in a half-standing position.

Such a division must of course be made, like all generalizations, on a purely arbitrary basis. As can be seen from the illustrations, several of the modest total of 42 positions treated in this book cannot be fitted into any of these categories; but by means of Illustrations A.B.C. and D. it can be seen that for many people they are transitions from one category to another; and by using these same illustrations one can come to some conclusion about the soundness of the principle on which the divisions have been made. At the same time these anatomical outlines of intercourse give certain guiding-lines for gauging the extent and intensity of the effect of stimulating the central erotogenic regions of both the man and the woman, which in the various positions can be achieved with a fair degree of probability. The sketches used show structural cross-sections of the sexual organs when together and also of the angle at which the penis is inserted in the vagina. The places marked with crosses indicate where the closest contact between the penis and the sides of the vagina will occur under normal anatomical conditions.

A. Sexual intercourse with the woman lying on her back and the man lying over her. The diagram shows the situation in which the woman lies with her knees drawn up to her chest. In this position the penis — the whole of it — can enter the vagina and at the same time a direct and powerful stimulation of the clitoris and the surrounding area is possible, since it is fixed between the symphysis pubis of the male and that of the female. Dependent on the individual woman's anatomical conditions this stimulation can be strengthened or weakened according as she lifts or lowers her legs. The way which is shown here, with the knees drawn up, is an ideal position for intercourse if one is hoping for pregnancy. The vagina provides in this way a very steep tube in which, after the man's orgasm, the semen collects and stays. For this purpose it is perhaps advisable to place a pillow under the woman's buttocks so that she can keep this position after ejaculation at least for a few minutes (5-10) and without any effort. This sketch corresponds to the illustration shown on page 37. For variations of this position refer to pages 27, 29, and 31.

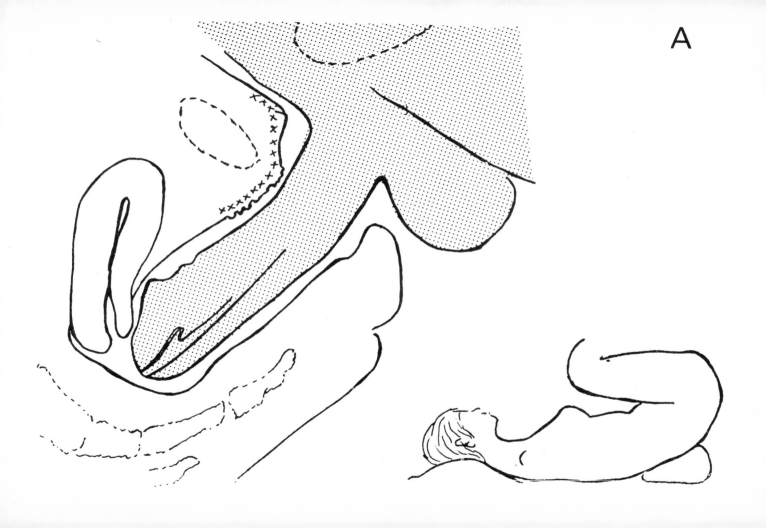

A

B. Intercourse with the woman lying on her stomach above the man. As the drawing shows, the possibilities of a direct stimulation of the area of the clitoris are good in this position too. Moreover in this position the woman is easily enabled to regulate the stimulation herself, as well as control the insertion of the penis. The man cannot move a great deal, but the position can be excellent for him too since the woman is able, by means of her thigh and pelvis muscles, to increase or decrease the pressure of the vagina on the penis just as she wishes. This position is not suitable for conception since the semen immediately after ejaculation will run straight out of the vagina. This position is also shown on page 39, and variations of it can be seen on pages 49, 51 and 53.

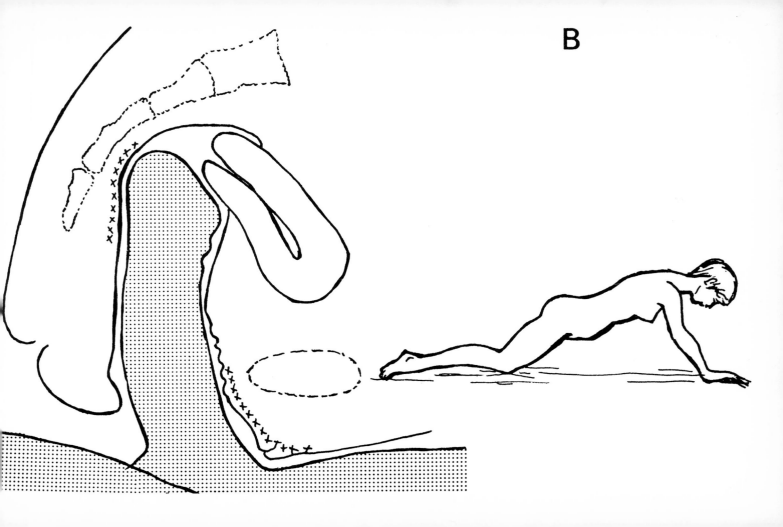

B

C. Intercourse with the penis entering from behind. In this position the introduction of the penis normally takes place at a fairly acute angle, with the result that the strongest point of contact is on the front part of the back wall of the vagina and on the back section of the front wall. This means that under normal anatomical conditions a direct excitement of the clitoris is not easy to achieve. The penis will usually be able to penetrate the full length of the vagina in this position, but it is an unsuitable one for conception since the semen can run out of the vagina. This position corresponds to the photos on pages 73, 75 and 77.

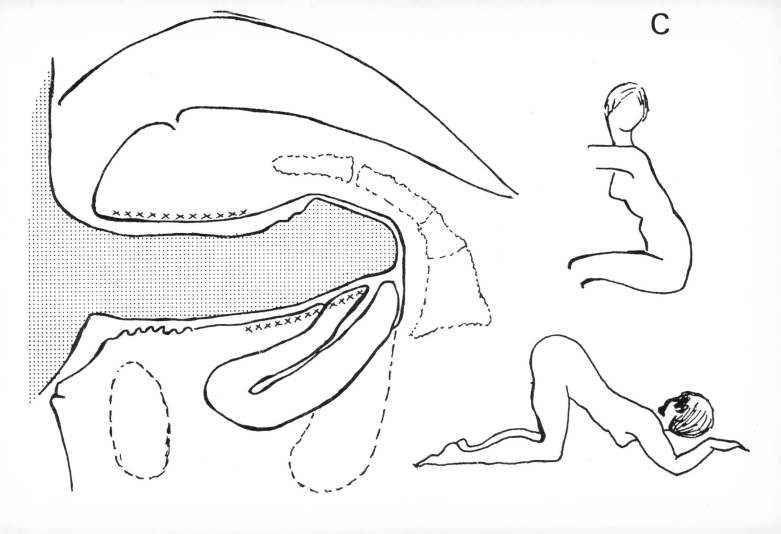

C

D. Intercourse in which the penis insertion is from the front, in a standing or half-standing position. As the drawing shows, positions based on this fundamental method facilitate a direct and powerful stimulation of the clitoris. Most men and women find this a very exciting position and both are able to make movements during intercourse in this way. The chances of a pregnancy are not high, since the vagina is turned at a slant towards the ground, so that when the penis is withdrawn most of the semen will probably go with it. The diagram refers to the photos on pages 85 and 103.

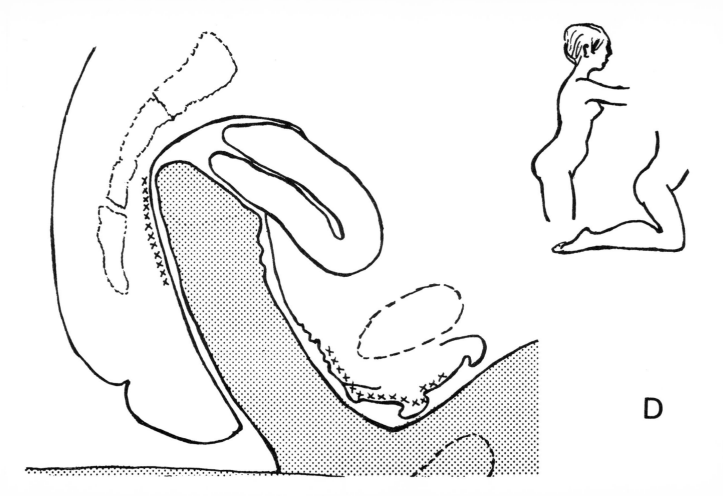

D

Positions

This is the position we normally think of as the "average" one. The fact that this position has been accepted for generations as the most usual one — and is probably still widespread today — is due in the first instance to two factors: the influence of the church and our defective knowledge of the sexual customs of other races and cultural patterns. Perhaps the reason is quite simply ignorance of one's own cultural background, since both in ancient Greece as well as in Rome the position, with the woman sitting astride the man, was the one preferred. According to Kinsey some of the inhabitants of the Pacific Islands, who knew nothing of the blessings of western civilzation before the 18th century, call this position the "missionary method". Some anthropologists believe that it derives from the cold northern regions, where intercourse normally took place under a number of thick coverings. In the Middle Ages the Catholic Church prohibited all other positions. However that may be, the position is quite a satisfying one even if somewhat monotonous if employed for any length of time. But its biggest disadvantage is that the woman is not allowed to make much movement of her own free will. Her hips are pinned down by the man's weight, making manual stimulation of both genitalia during intercourse quite impossible. However, this method is best during the last stages of coition immediately before and after the man's orgasm, since it allows the man considerable freedom of movement. At the same time of course the fact that the woman is being firmly held can have an even more stimulating effect, both on the man and the woman.

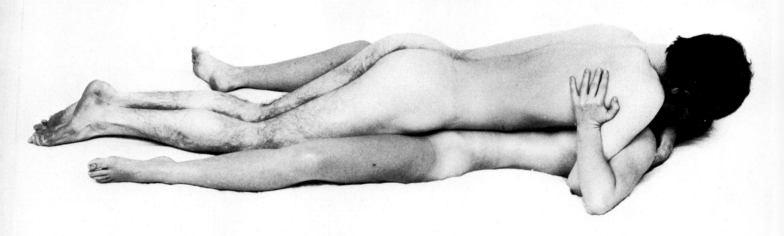

This attitude is a direct variation of our "normal" position. The woman here is likewise held more or less firmly, with the result that a manual stimulation of the sex organs of both is not easy to carry out; but it is possible for the man to caress the woman's breasts. At the same time there is a rhymic rubbing between the male pubic bone and the upper section of the woman's labia (i.e. the vulva lips) and therefore stimulation of the clitoris too. The insertion of the penis can take place with little or no trouble in any position in which the woman is lying on her back with legs wide apart. The method shown here, however, does give the best chance of an unhindered introduction of the penis into the vagina. The position is therefore one to recommend if the man is not very experienced sexually or the woman is a virgin.

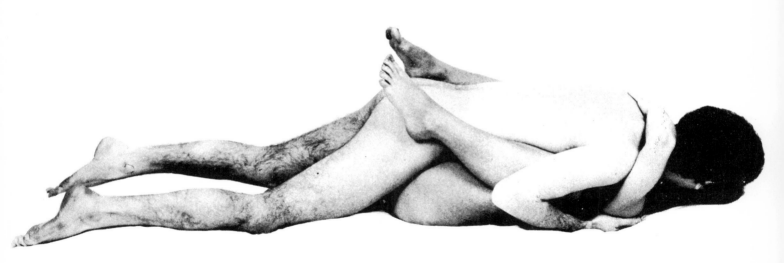

A strongly erotic stimulus upon the male is often the result of simply seeing the woman in this position, as her legs are widely spread apart and the vulva lips, both inner and outer, are opened, thus exposing the entrance to the vagina and the clitoris. This greatly helps the insertion of the penis if the woman's vagina is unusually narrow. It can at the same time bring about friction between the entire area round the clitoris and the pubic bone and pubic hair. The woman is unable to move much in this attitude but it is possible for her to increase the effect of the man's movements during intercourse by a swaying motion in the lower part of her body. It is presumably the position affording the deepest penetration by the penis, so it is a favourable one to adopt if the male organ is either rather short or if the woman is strongly stimulated by the full penetration and the resultant widening deep inside the vagina.

This position is far less tiring for both the man and the woman than the two previous ones. Although it does not offer much chance of manual stimulation during intercourse it has many other advantages. If the penis is comparatively small or the vagina rather large the woman's thighs, being firmly pressed together, exercise a constant pressure on the penis and at the same time this can be of great importance if the man's erection is rather weak or if he experiences any difficulty in reaching orgasm or ejaculating. Simultaneously the increased friction between the penis and the vaginal walls and lips means that the woman, too, is more strongly stimulated than she is in the three preceding positions. Finally it is possible for both man and woman to effect a certain direct stimulation of the clitoris, since the top part of the root of the penis can be brought into more or less direct contact with the clitoris area. This effect is most easily obtained if the man pushes himself towards the woman's shoulders and head.

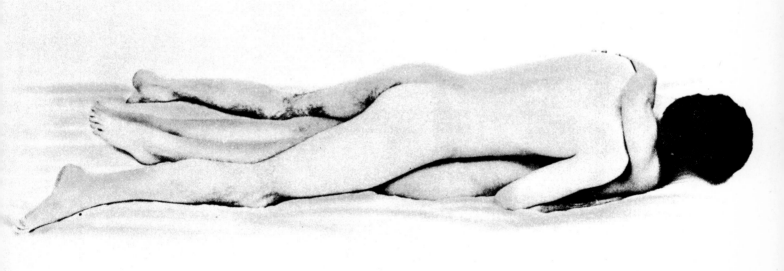

A fairly comfortable position for both. It allows an unhindered insertion of the penis and makes it possible for both of them to stimulate the breasts and clitoris during intercourse. This may certainly be advisable in many cases since this method probably has no strong effect upon the lips or clitoris or upon the penis. A variation of this method can be obtained by the woman pressing her thighs together and by the man leaning forward over her body instead of kneeling between her legs.

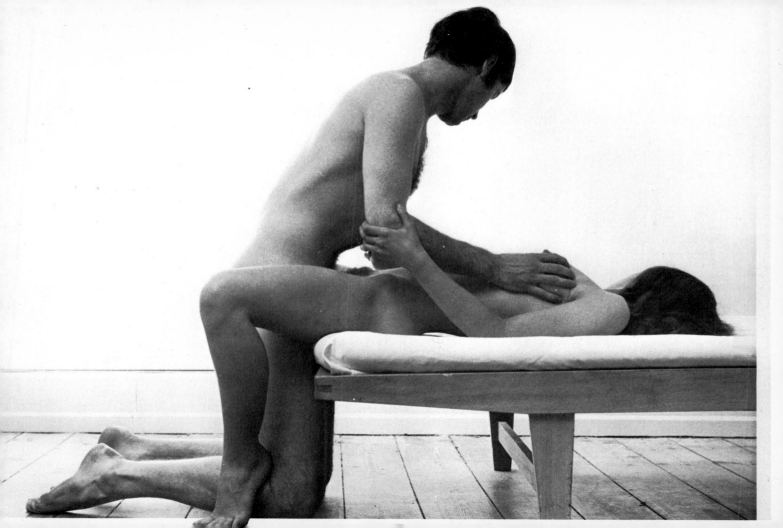

The position shown here demands of both partners a considerable agility and elasticity and it is one which undoubtedly includes factors of a very marked psychological nature. From a physiological point of view it is a position which is not highly effective as a stimulus. Because of the angle at which the penis (assuming normal anatomical conditions in both partners) enter the vagina there is probably only an indirect stimulation of the clitoris region. Furthermore a full penetration by the penis is hindered in this position by the woman's coccyx, and neither the man nor the woman can stimulate manually. Movements during intercourse are comparatively limited in extent and speed. A transfer from this position to the "normal" one can be effected if the woman allows her legs to slip down over the man's shoulders and on to the bed.

A number of classical authors maintain that this method of intercourse is excellent for allowing the woman to satisfy herself in her own way. This can be challenged perhaps but there is no doubt that it is one of the positions offering the woman the maximum manoeuvrability and thus gives the best chance of her being able to adapt the stimulus to her wishes and requirements.

The woman can control the depth of penetration, the strength of contact between the male pubis and her clitoris area, and the tempo and rhythm of the movements she want to have. In cases where the penis is not quite erect — whether because the man's sexual excitement is not as strong as the woman's or because he had his orgasm before the woman had hers completely — the woman can be sexually satisfied by using the penis root, which is stiffer than the rest, to excite the inner lips and the clitoris. This position also lets the woman masturbate with her hands; or the man can stimulate her breasts while she is masturbating.

This position is largely identical with the former, the chief difference being that the woman can lean back and support herself on the man's bent legs. This lessens the chance of direct contact between clitoris and male pubis, but on the other hand the man or woman has a much better chance of being able to excite the clitoris or area round it by using the hands. The position is certainly one of the most suitable in cases where the man is satisfied before the woman and the latter wishes to be able to feel the penis in the vagina until she has obtained her satisfaction by masturbating.

This variation is different from the preceding ones, especially in that it allows the woman to increase the pressure on the penis and thus to excite the man more. The position has all the advantages which characterize the two preceding ones.

Intercourse from behind is also possible if the woman sits astride the man, who lies in this position on his back, either with his legs stretched out or, as shown here, bent in order to support the woman. The insertion of the penis is facilitated if the woman bends forward. After the penis has entered she can either squat down or support herself on her knees; and either the man or she herself can carry out the movements, dependent on the position she adopts. The woman can herself decide the depth of the penetration, depending on whether she leans forward on to the man's knees or backwards towards his chest. The man is unable to stimulate the clitoris region directly but on the other hand the woman is free to excite both clitoris and the inner lips.

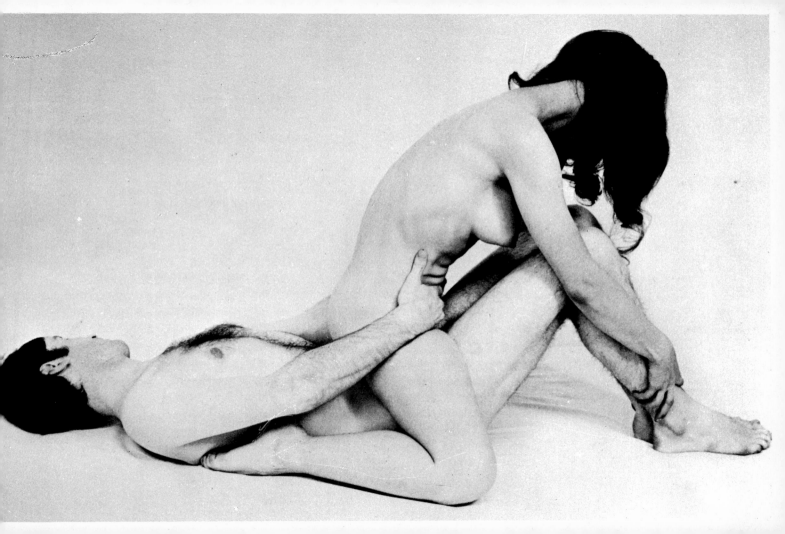

This method requires a fair amount of room, so a rather broad bed, or the floor, is advisable. To get into this position the man lifts his legs towards his chest, spreading his knees as far apart as possible. The woman places herself astride the lower side of the thighs and the insertion of the penis can now be effected without any trouble. The woman then leans against the man's body so that he can put his legs round her back and thus hold her with his calves and thighs. The man is thus enabled to bring about a swaying movement from side to side which increases stimulus.

This picture portrays the riding position in its recumbent aspect. In this position, as in most of those in which the man lies on his back beneath the woman, the woman can by and large decide how deep the penetration is to be and she can also determine the rhythm of the movements. If the erection is strong the woman's weight will press the penis down a little and this causes the pulling of the inner lips by the penis, which is usual during intercourse. Indirectly this heightens the stimulation of the clitoris.

By means of a small change in the preceding position the woman can, if desired, have the strongest possible stimulation of the clitoris. If the woman lies quite straight between the man's thighs and with her legs closed, she can by means of her strong thigh muscles increase the pressure which the vaginal walls have on the penis. This has an immediate effect in that the pulling of the inner lips by the penis — and other movements during intercourse — is increased; which also serves as a means of stimulating the clitoris indirectly. As contact between the male and female pubic bones is very close in this position it means that an intense and direct excitement of the clitoris and the whole pubic bone region is feasible. The whole length of the penis will thus be pressed against the front wall of the vagina, and closely. At the same time the penis can be inserted rather deeply, which enables both man and woman to have a sensation of the deepest possible union as a result of this extra stimulation. It is important both physically and psychologically that the couple are facing each other and are holding each other firmly.

As already mentioned it is not unusual for both man and woman to try to increase sexual excitement just before orgasm by flexing body and leg muscles. This happens unconsciously as a result of heightened sexual excitement but can be used as a conscious means of encouraging orgasm. In this method, which is almost identical with the two previous ones, the sexual intercourse movements will bring about almost unavoidably such a convulsive flexing of all the body muscles; and since the woman in this position lies on the man's legs with her own legs stretched out but closed, like his, then her weight will be enough to hold the man quite firmly. The man's share in the sexual motions is chiefly that he can lift his hips, and therefore the penis too, pushing them up and towards the lower part of the woman's body. A convulsive movement of the thigh, belly and back muscles thus arises. This exertion will help to increase the man's sexual excitement very considerably. As was the case in the previous variations it is also possible here for the woman to guide the extent and pace of the intercourse movements. It also demands a considerable exertion of her muscles if she is to carry out such motions and at the same time maintain her balance on the man. As a fair amount of direct and indirect stimulation of the clitoris and lips is possible in this position too it is very likely that this method is a very suitable one for obtaining simultaneous orgasm.

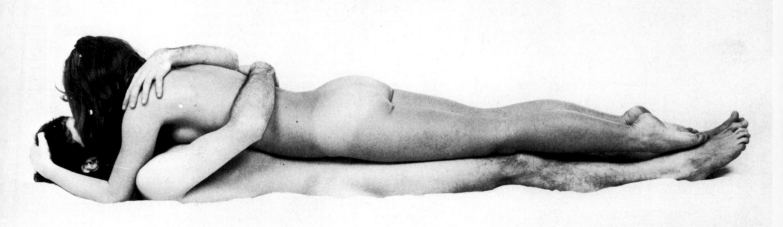

The method shown here is really a combination of the "riding" position and its derivatives, all of which have been already indicated. Without interrupting coition one can adopt this position directly, or with a certain amount of agility obtain it from one of the previous positions. This is achieved by the woman drawing up her knees under her so that she is crouching over the man, who then straightens himself and supports his body against hers, while she lets her legs slip behind his back. The same method can be employed if the couple are already in the "riding" position, but it is one which does not allow much special movement and has no particular effect, as intensive stimulation of the genitalia is hardly possible. And yet the close embrace and the strong feeling of intimate union will probably be for most people a source of intense erotic happiness.

The position shown in this picture, where one lies on one's side, c..n be arrived at, without disturbing intercourse, by the two people leaving the "normal" method, where the woman lies on her back, and sliding on to one of their sides. But intercourse can be started in this way too; in which case it is most likely necessary for the woman to lift or bend a leg so that the penis can be inserted. When insertion has taken place intercourse can either be concluded in this position or the couple can transfer from it to another one. The main difference between the method shown here and the normal one is that both man and woman can stimulate the erotogenic zones or the sexual organs better; which can be done by the uppermost arm as it is free.

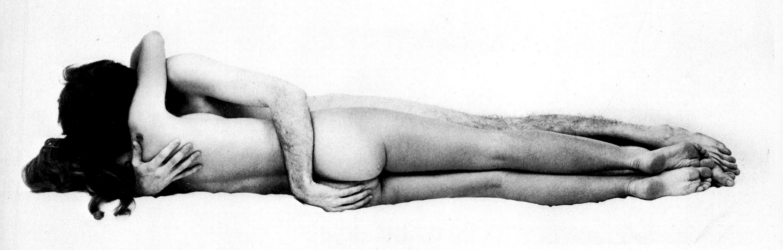

This position requires a relatively small amount of muscular exertion, and because of the angle at which the insertion of the penis takes place it is suitable where one of the couple is either very strong or is pregnant. The method does not allow much freedom of movement but as one arm is free there can be mutual manual stimulation. Jerome and Julia Rainer mention in "Variety and Change in Sexual Life" a variation of this position (see page 63) which permits both partners a somewhat greater freedom of movement. In this position the man places himself at a right angle to the woman but they still face each other. The woman lies on her side but spreads and bends her legs so that her knees touch the man's armpits. In this way the man is in a better position to carry out active movements, in the course of which he can manually stimulate breasts, thighs and buttocks.

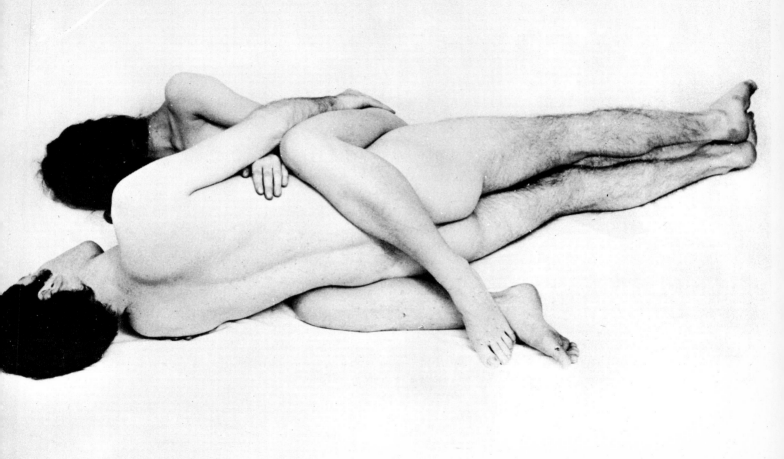

This position differs from the previous ones chiefly in that the former have the couple lying on their sides and facing each other, whereas now the man can alter the angle of insertion of his penis into the vagina by adjusting his position parallel to the woman's body. After insertion he is therefore able to control the pressure which the root of the penis has upon the front part of the vagina, on the lips and thus on the whole area of the clitoris. The method does at least allow in the case of some women a direct stimulation of the clitoris.

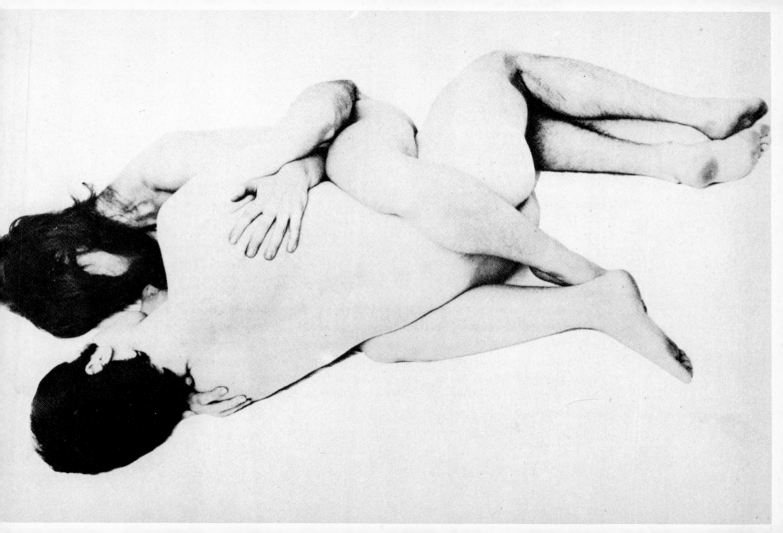

This position corresponds principally to the variation discussed on page 58. But there is a fundamental difference in that the man in this position can make strong pushing movements which he can increase by using his hands to press the woman's buttocks against his hips. As in the three previous positions contact between the man's pubic bone and the clitoris is hardly possible here either, so there is no immediate excitement of the latter organ. On the other hand these positions are comfortable for both and allow a direct manual stimulation of the clitoris region.

A particularly suitable method — like the earlier ones — in the last months of pregnancy, when the insertion of the penis is rendered difficult by the woman's increased size. Its most advantageous factor is that the man can directly stimulate the woman's breasts and clitoris region without any trouble, while drawing the woman's body firmly towards his own. Stimulation like this will in no way hinder the couple's freedom to move as they wish; and as a result the effect on the woman of these stimuli can be greater in this position than in most of the others.

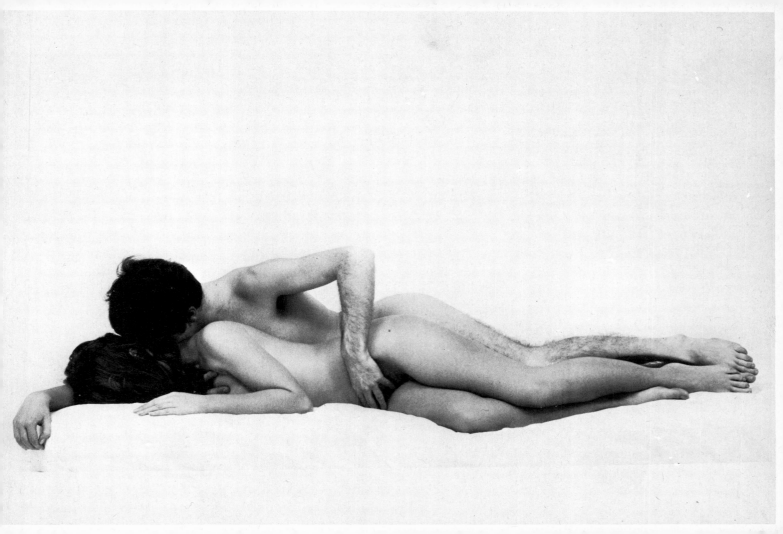

The method indicated here must be regarded as something of an oddity but has been included chiefly because of the change and variation possible. Introduction of the penis is not easy but can be assisted by the woman raising her upper leg until the penis is inside. It is not a position allowing much movement but does not rule out a mutual, manual stimulation, and can if necessary act as a stimulus should the erection be weak, since the penis is forced downwards once it is held inside the vagina and as a result the large veins on the lower section of the organ are firmly squeezed together. This considerably decreases the flow of blood away from the penis, so that there is a heavy accumulation of blood in it and therefore a stronger erection.

A position in which the penis is inserted from behind; helped considerably if the man has one or more pillows supporting his back. To get into this position the woman places herself astride the man, with her face towards his feet. If the penis is already inside then the woman can lie on her stomach between the man's legs, and is thus able to stretch out her own. The man can sit up to some extent, using his hands to draw her hips towards him. If increased movement is desired this can be done by each partner taking the wrist of the other and alternately pressing the other towards him — or herself.

This one refers to the position on page 65, where the couple lie on their sides. As in that position it is possible here also for both man and woman to excite the breasts and the clitoris area manually. The woman, unlike the man, cannot in this position make any particularly strong movements but as it is probably one of the commonest methods both partners have very considerable choice in the matter of intensive and varied stimulation. If the insertion of the penis is made difficult by the vaginal opening being turned towards the front a pillow can be placed under the woman's hips and this usually solves the problem.

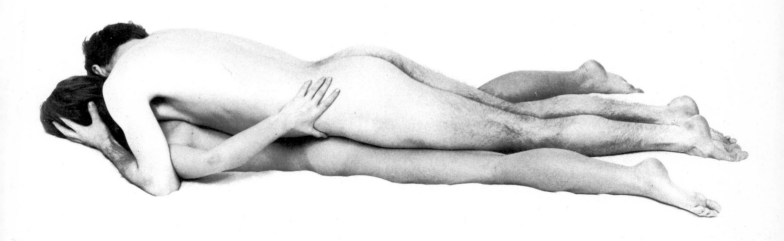

In cases where there is difficulty in getting the penis to enter the vagina in the position just shown it can be helped if the couple adopt the method illustrated here. If the woman lies on her knees the vaginal opening will be turned straight back towards the man standing behind her. If the woman lies with her legs also firmly pressed together there is nothing to hinder insertion of the penis usually and the woman can let herself slide down on to her stomach until they are in the position discussed on the previous page. Intercourse is possible in this attitude too, and it is one which distinguishes itself in several ways. It is ideal for the woman since by pressing her legs together she can stimluate the clitoris indirectly still more, thus helping the effect which the penis has already exerted on the inner lips. She can also increase the man's movements by swaying back and forth on her hands and knees. Lastly the man is able to stimulate the clitoris directly with one of his hands, while with the other he can draw the woman's buttocks towards his body. If he likes he can also hold the woman's body with his hands, and quite firmly; at the same time he can make strong, thrusting movements of the hips. In this position the penis attains maximum penetration, which of course is a further stimulus for both.

This method and the following two variations correspond on the whole to the one represented on page 73, and is especially suitable in cases of hastily improvised sex. The same conditions as those mentioned on page 72 apply in this technique, which has the unqualified advantage of being realised with the minimum of undressing or other preparations and it can be varied in a number of ways. The woman can support herself on the back of a chair or something similar; or by putting her hands on her knees if the intercourse is taking place in the open. This position is therefore independent of all conditions except of course the presence and the willingness of both partners.

This attitude is a variation of the two previous ones, and like these it has several practical advantages. It is extremely handy if the woman is very strong and thus the penetration is difficult from the front. The man can similarly make powerful thrusts which the woman can react to by rocking to and fro in the same rhythm as the man's. At the same time the position, and the others of this nature, encourage the man to stroke the woman's breasts and thus increase the stimuli. The clitoris region can also be excited in this position.

This method differs from the preceding ones only by the man holding the woman's closed legs between his own, which significantly heightens the stimulus for both: a position to be recommended in cases where the penis, compared with the vagina, is relatively small.

Intercourse in a standing position and with the penis insertion from the back can be very difficult and sometimes impossible, especially if the couple are not of approximately the same size. In cases where penis insertion is difficult the woman can help by bending forward a little and by lifting a leg sideways. Once the penis is inside she can extend her leg again a little and straighten up again, after which the intercourse can be consummated. As is the case in the other positions where the penis enters from behind the man can stimulate the woman's genitals by manual manipulation.

This position can be arrived at from various starting positions. At first the woman can lie on her back and the man can then lift her up by clasping her round the hips. If the woman is sufficiently athletic she can let herself slip backwards from a kneeling attitude until her shoulders and neck are touching the mattress or the floor. Lastly she can, given sufficient elasticity, form a bridge or span and the penis can then be introduced. In all cases the man will probably have to support her body with his hands under her hips if the position is to be held for any length of time. Even so, the position is a very tiring one and most women are not likely to want to remain in it throughout the intercourse. But it is fine for variety and it is better than the majority of positions in several respects. For the man it is a strong stimulus just to see the woman's body bent in an arch and secondly — perhaps the biggest advantage — this position itself will force the woman to flex her muscles to the utmost; a fact which she often uses consciously as a means of increasing sexual excitement at the climax. So for experienced people very familiar with each other's sexual rhythms and able to know when the woman's orgasm is coming this position is probably the most rewarding.

This method requires a soft layer of some sort under the knees if the position is to be held more than a few moments. It is reached by the woman spreading her thighs and by the man either drawing himself towards her or letting the woman slide forwards until his knees are lying between her thighs. Intercourse can now be carried out or the couple can let themselves move to one side or the other, just as they can also adopt a position where either the man or the woman (with the other partner on top) lies on his or her back. Direct stimulation of the clitoris is possible, irrespective of the size of the couple. Direct stimulation will be at its strongest if the man is somewhat bigger than the woman, since in this case the penis is pressed downwards by the woman's weight. That part of the penis left outside the vagina has close contact with the lips in their fullest extent. This is easiest if the penis is not yet fully erect, since the organ then more intimately follows the folds of the female genitalia.

This method presupposes in the couple a certain strength and suppleness. It is carried out by the woman placing herself on her knees (if intercourse is not taking place in a bed then this positions also needs a pillow or something similar laid under the knees) and bending forward, at the same time supporting herself on her hands, while the man, lying on his knees in front of her, places his penis in the vagina. He can now lean against her if she is strong enough to take his weight and force of the movements. He can also stay sitting upright, drawing the woman to him with rhythmical movements, made by holding her round the hips. Here too, as in the previous position, a direct stimulation of the clitoris region is feasible if the man is as big as or bigger than the woman.

This variation is easiest on a fairly hard underlay — the floor would be suitable. Both partners open the thighs so that the hips of one can clasp the hips of the other. Penis insertion is easiest if the woman's legs lie over those of the man's; the sex movements occurring because the lower part of the body pushes against that of the partner. Not a very tiring position but there cannot be much intense, physiological stimulation, effective manual manipulation being limited because both partners are either supporting themselves with their hands or using the latter to hold on to each other and thus keep their balance. But as it is one of the few positions where the union of the sexual organs and movements is visible for both the purely mental effect of this may in turn contribute significantly to an increase of sexual excitement.

Advantages of a purely practical nature, and there are several, can be derived from intercourse in a sitting position. It is easy to carry out without much undressing or other preparation. This first variation of intercourse in a sitting position is probably the commonest. But this does not mean that it is necessarily the best method for obtaining effective sexual stimulation. In this first variation the man sits on a chair and the woman sits straddled over him, at the same time supporting her feet on the floor or on the rungs of a chair. In this position it is the woman who makes the sex movements. The chances of an intense sexual stimulation — by the hands for instance — are not very good, but a close embrace is possible and will probably attract most people because of the element of variety.

Intercourse in a sitting position — second variation. In this one there is better chance of intense stimulation than in the version just shown. Now the woman can close her legs and thus the vagina produces greater pressure on the penis, which then has the double effect of increasing the stimuli for both. If the man opens his thighs the woman can press her body closer and thus the penis will push further into the vagina. This heightens the feeling that the latter organ is being fully extended, which for many women is a sure method of increasing sexual excitement. Furthermore the man is unhindered in his manual manipulation of breasts, etc.

The third and last variation of intercourse in a sitting position. If the man has a strong erection this position allows complete penetration of the vagina. If the erection is weaker, or if the penis compared with the vagina is not particularly long there can be an increased degree of penetration if the man moves slightly forward and downwards on the chair so that his hip-joint is partly straightened out. In this way there can be maximum contact as well as deepest possible penetration. Besides this the woman may, thanks to the strong thigh-muscles, clasp the penis more firmly, with the effect mentioned on page 92. Although this position does not permit either partner any especially active movements it does perhaps offer to a greater extent than·the previous one a simultaneous manual stimulation of the woman's erotogenic zones, among other things because the position itself has a stimulating effect.

The next three positions to be dealt with all require that the woman lies on her back on some object or other — a table, say — which is at hip height. In this first example she lies with her legs wide apart and loosely hanging down, so that the man, standing upright between her thighs, can easily insert his penis. Movement is made by the man, either by pushing the hips rhythmically or by drawing the woman to him in a rhythmic motion, which he can do by clasping her hips or thighs.

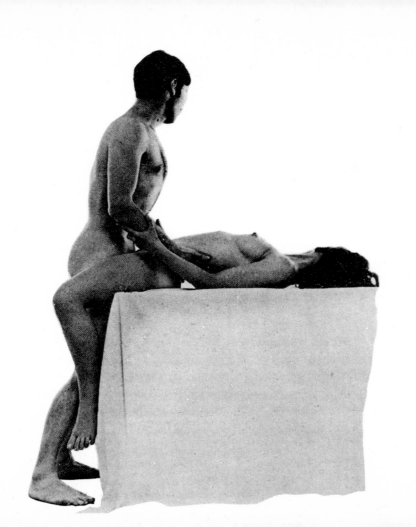

This variation differs chiefly from the former one in that a deeper penetration is possible if the woman lifts her legs up whilst she is lying down on her back. In this position she can also control the sex movements by using her calves and ankles to draw the lower part of the man's body towards her, thus influencing the pace and intensity of movement. If she likes, the man can manually manipulate the whole pubic region and clitoris without any disturbance of the sex movements or lessening of tension and do it without any difficulty.

This final variation will probably evoke in most people the strongest sexual stimulus. Because of·the strong muscles of her thighs and buttocks the woman can tighten her hold upon the penis, and while the man leans forward over the woman he assists the deepest possible penetration. The more powerfully the penis is held the stronger is its effect upon the inner lips, which means that the clitoris is indirectly stimulated all the more.

Intercourse standing up. A prerequisite is that both partners are of the same approximate size. If the woman is bigger than the man she may bend her knees a little in order to obtain complete penetration, in which case the insertion is not difficult. If the man is considerably larger than the woman then insertion and intercourse are possible only with a certain amount of difficulty. To facilitate insertion the woman lifts a leg, turning it sideways a little so that the man can introduce the penis, after which both legs can be used in support. The vagina then clasps the penis firmly and the woman uses her whole pelvis to make fairly strong sexual movements without letting the male organ slip out of her body. In this position the woman can herself produce a very strong stimulation of the inner lips and also of the clitoris in some cases, by leaning forward a little and bending her knees slightly if the partners are of the same size. It is a tiring method if kept up for any length of time but owing to the muscular exertion it can considerably increase sexual excitement. From this position the couple can continue intercourse undisturbed in either a sitting or a lying position or, if necessary, they can use as a transitional stage the method indicated on the next page.

An apparently great amount of exertion on the part of both the man and the woman is demanded by this position but once it has been reached it is not particularly tiring because the man and the woman distribute the load, so to speak, equally between them. The simplest method for approaching it is for the man and woman to stand opposite each other and after insertion the woman holds the man's neck and he lifts her up by placing his hands under her thighs; after which she crosses her legs behind his back and presses her thighs around his hips. Insertion takes place as in the variation just shown, but if both partners are relatively agile the insertion can be done after the woman has adopted the half-sitting, half-hanging position with legs crossed behind the man's back. In this position the man will be able to move the woman back and forth on his hands and also control the intensity of the movements whilst guiding the swaying motion and the tempo. In erotic literature this method has had a great deal of praise and once into the position then intercourse may be continued standing up, walking or, if you like, even dancing. Whether in a sitting or lying position intercourse can be continued undisturbed. It is a method affording almost no manual stimulation but one which will seem to most people so fascinating that this defect is completely cancelled out by the purely mental uplift gained.

A continuation of the previous position. The woman loosens her hold on the man's neck and leans backwards till her shoulders are pressing against a wall or the like. If the man uses his hands to support the woman's thighs in this position he is enabled to make thrusting movements with his hips. The principle difference between this and the previous position is that the woman now has both arms free, thus permitting her to stimulate manually both her own genitalia and those of the man.

Oriental literature is well known because of its many textbooks on love. The eastern epicureans went to endless lengths to bring change and subtlety into their sex-life. When all other possibilities were exhausted they were able to employ pulleys attached to the ceiling etc., making an aerial art of love. The method represented here is taken from classical textbooks on sex, where it occurs under numerous headings and descriptions e.g. Climbing Vine or the Lotus Position. It can be reached in the following way: with the couple facing each other the woman puts her right arm over the man's left shoulder, supporting his back with her left arm above his hips. The man then puts his right arm over the woman's left shoulder, after which she raises her right leg and bends it so that the knee is turned sideways. Insertion of the penis now takes place, with the woman pressing her calf against the man's thigh while the man puts his left arm round her back and just above the hips so as to support her. Finally the man places his left leg in an appropriate position against the back part of the woman's thigh and proper intercourse can now proceed. This position is inadvisable for those who are insufficiently gymnastic and supple; and since the description of it is complicated it is probably just as difficult to put into practice. For those with enough spirit, suppleness and energy let it be understood, as is clear from the picture, that it *can* in fact be done like this.

There are many men, and maybe women too, who even if fairly well experienced sexually have never had an opportunity of making a close examination of the vagina. Unlike the penis the vagina cannot be seen immediately and in any case the sex-life of many takes place in the dark or under bedclothes. This picture shows the whole vulva (the word comes from Latin). The outer lips are closed in the mid-position under normal circumstances so that the other structures are covered. The inner lips are situated immediately inside the outer ones and in this picture are held aside so that one can see the vaginal orifice. The large outer lips form at the top a triangular fold of skin — the prepuce of the clitoris — which covers the clitoris, the woman's most sensitive sexual organ. This can be clearly seen in the picture. As mentioned in the text the clitoris withdraws towards the top during the plateau-stage of sexual excitement so that it is covered by the triangular piece of skin and thus inaccessible to direct contact. Stimulation of the inner lips or the whole region round the clitoris is perfectly adequate in this situation for producing the woman's orgasm. In the middle of the picture can be seen the urethra orifice and underneath it the opening of the vagina itself.

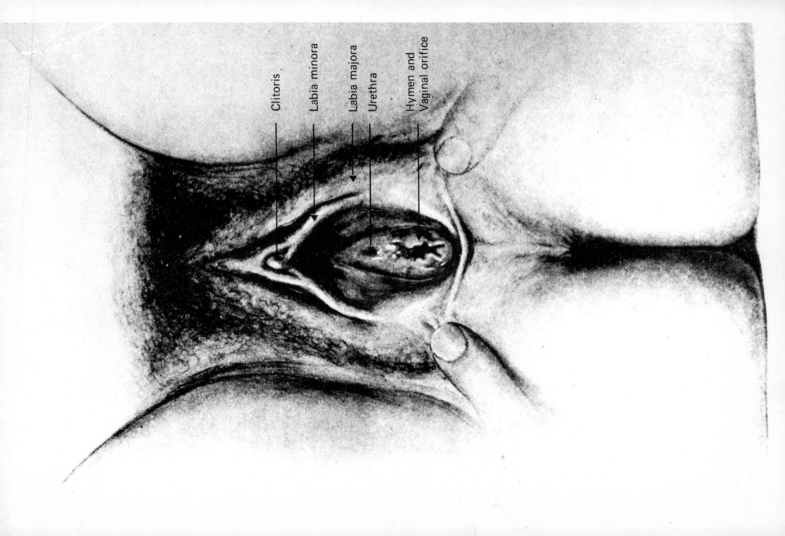

Clitoris

Labia minora

Labia majora

Urethra

Hymen and
Vaginal orifice

The Sexual Organs

The human sexual organs or genitalia have a number of functions. Like the digestive system it is extremely complicated and when it is not functioning properly can seriously prejudice a large part of one's life; but as its best it can be vital for the promotion of a great deal of happiness. Just as the digestive system has a number of organs supplying the various parts of the digestive and absorbtive systems in the best possible way so too does the human reproductive method possess a number of individual organs. Together they form a unity, the function of which is to ensure the continuity of man as a species: this is its most important function. But here the comparison with the digestive system stops, because while each man can deal with his own digestion he cannot undertake his own reproduction using solely *his* resources. Such a man never existed. Our reproductive system is split in two, the man having one and the woman the other part, and thus it is up to us to find a partner. In fact we must if, the system is to function sensibly. This division has brought problems with it in the course of time and it would probably be impossible to find a single person who has not had the opportunity of experiencing such problems within himself, at least to some degree.

If one considers the problem objectively it should really not have so many complications. The man supplies the sperm fertilizing the egg in the uterus (womb) after which the unborn child (called the foetus or embryo) lies well protected in the uterus for the first nine months, until its development has progressed so far that it has a chance of survival in the world outside. This process is of course extremely complicated but only a small number of the problems which can arise while this is going on cannot be solved by those who are not experts; and as is known by everybody it is not only the doctors who have sexual problems. Human beings are by nature lazy and sex demands a considerable amount of energy; if we had no sex instinct it is hardly likely that we would venture upon it. This is one of the most deeply rooted elements of the human psyche; the sex instinct can take various forms and can be directed towards various objects but it is quite literally always present. By this means nature guarantees that we use our reproductive system efficiently; and the second important function of the sexual organs is to ensure that this urge finds satisfaction.

To a certain extent the sex urge is determined by purely physiological means. Perhaps this applies primarily to the male, whose testicles in his reproductive years produce sperms almost incessantly. The sperm or semen collects in the seminal vesicles, which it leaves via the penis during sexual intercourse or masturbation. If the man has no intercourse and does not masturbate the semen will nevertheless still be emitted when the seminal vesicles are filled to a certain level. This reflex action often takes place at night and is frequently accompanied by erotic dreams. Which means that the purely physiological reaction going on in the vesicles causes other reactions of a purely *psychological* nature. For most people it is the mental side of the sex urge which is the strongest motivating factor and at the same time the source of the biggest problems of sexual life. Most sexual problems can be solved only with the aid of psychiatry, but innumerable quite ordinary people who think that they do not need psychiatric help nevertheless have problems in their sex life. Whoever reads the correspondence columns of newspapers and magazines knows that such problems are many-sided and varied. On a rough analysis they can be split into two main categories — the moral and the purely practical problems.

The first category lies outside the scope of this book; it is up to the individual to decide what is moral or immoral. But in the second class the cause of a large part of the purely practical problems connected with sex is ignorance. Sexology — the scientific exploration of sexual life — is still a relatively young branch of research and furthermore one which often encounters prejudices and rejection when it comes up against authority. At best the scientific research into sexual life is considered with scepticism and at worst it is positively marked down as the work of the devil. Only the past 10 or 15 years have furthered the work considerably and the purely practical results are noticed only gradually by the bulk of the populace.

This book will perhaps be able to contribute to the solution of some problems to do with sex, but its chief aim is to encourage people who already have a regular sexual relationship and wish to bring change and variety into it so as to increase their happiness as much as possible.

The Sexual Reactions

The sex organs are the means placed at our disposal for satisfying the sex instinct, but we cannot expect any satisfying results if we possess no thorough knowledge of how the sex organs function. Familiarity with the instruments at hand is as necessary here as in any field of endeavour.

The two American research workers, Dr. William H. Masters and the psychologist Virginia E.

Johnson have done a vast amount of work in this field in the course of about ten years. They have studied the course of several thousand sexual reactions in their laboratories at the biological institute in St. Louis. In order to get a clear, comprehensive view of what happens when a human being reacts sexually they have divided the process into four phases. These four phases comprise the whole cycle in the sex organs and are briefly outlined here.

The first of the four phases — the excitement — begins the moment there is any stimulation at all; and this can be either of a physiological nature or psychological. So that means either the sex organs being stimulated by touch, or that one has erotic visions or sees a sex partner who causes the excitement. The second stage is called the "plateau phase" and is reached when the stimulus is carried to the point of orgasm. If the stimulus does not stop then the plateau-phase is replaced by the orgasm-phase, which as far as emission is concerned lasts only a few seconds. The last stage is the phase of relaxation which starts immediately after the orgasm and lasts until the last signs of excitement in the sex organs have faded. By their laboratory experiments Masters and Johnson have ascertained that the sex organs go through quite definite reactions which are basically the same, from one case of sex stimulus and satisfaction to the next. They were also able to observe that these reactions were the same no matter whether the stimulus was from intercourse, masturbation, erotic phantasies or any other kind of sex stimulus.

From a purely physiological point of view it means that sexual excitement — orgasm — which one can experience through intercourse, masturbation or any other form of sexual intimacy is thus the same. The body's reactions are the same.

Here the male and female organs and the reactions arising in them during sex stimulus are briefly described. In order to get an idea of how the reactions occur they will be considered with the Masters and Johnson reaction cycle. But it is important to make it clear that these reactions occur in the same sequence and intensity however they are aroused.

The Male Sex Organs

The male genitalia consist of the scrotum, with its testicles and epididymis, the spermatic cord leading from the testicles to the vesicles; and the penis with its urethra, through which the semen during orgasm is emitted. These organs all have some part or other to play in the pattern of sexual reactions.

In the first phase of stimulation the initial sign of excitement is erection of the penis. Diagrams 1 and 2 show respectively a section lengthwise and a cross-section of the penis, which is connected with the ilium (hip-bone) by a number of ligaments and muscles while the penis proper (corpus) begins underneath and behind the scrotum. As is clear from the second illustration the body of the penis consists of three separate elements (corpora) which are held together by small fibres or connective tissue. The two upper and largest of these erectile bodies are called the corpora cavernosa while the smallest and lowest one is known as the corpus spongiosus. These names refer to the fact that all three parts of the penis are filled with cavities which in the normal position of the organ are closed; but during the erection they are filled with blood so that the whole organ becomes hard and stiff. Under the top two corpora there is the urethra which is connected at the back with both the (urine) bladder and the vesicles. Right at the back of the urethra lies the prostate gland, the principle function of which is to surround the urethra so that no urine escapes except during micturition. The prostate is therefore responsible for ensuring that urine and semen are not mixed together during ejaculation. The extreme end of the penis — the glans — has a very thin skin which contains numerous nerve-endings and is the most sensitive part of the whole organ to touch.

The penis can be brought into the erect position through psychological means alone, such as by reading pornography, having sexual phantasies or by seeing an attractive partner — these are usually enough to cause an erection in a healthy man disposed towards sex — or the erection can also be the result of a physical influence; though it is probably often difficult to distinguish between a psychogenic and a physiological stimulus if, for example, the erection is caused by touching the penis.

It is a commonly held view that the size of the penis is an indication of the man's virility. This supposition is probably incorrect, as none of the experiments undertaken hitherto could establish any connection between virility and size of the penis. The two American workers already mentioned investigated the relationship between the size of the penis in a normally relaxed and also in an excited condition. They found that the length of a normally slack penis can vary from 5 — 6 centimetres up to 10 — 12. The investigation also showed that a penis which in the usual relaxed state is bigger than average grows during its erection proportionately less than a penis does which in the relaxed state is below average size. So a small penis grows during its erection more than a larger one, and there is moreover some doubt as to whether the size of the penis plays a decisive role when it comes to the question of a man's ability to satisfy his partner. The vagina is so elastic that even an abnormally large one can clasp the penis relatively firmly; and similarly even the smallest vagina can be stretched enough to take an unusually large penis. Here it might be mentioned that during birth the vagina has to be stretched so much that it must be wide enough for the child's head. The tissue is so elastic that the size of the penis is not a major issue.

Apart from the penis, which in most men is the organ having the highest sensitivity, the scrotum and the area around the anus also possess a high degree of sensitivity to the sexual stimuli.

It is presumably not unusual for a man to have an orgasm if the very sensitive skin of the scrotum and the area between this and the anus is massaged or stroked. Concurrently with the erection of the penis there is a thickening of the scrotal skin, caused by the latter now having an increased blood-supply. In the plateau phase there is an increased thickening of the penis and the testicles are enlarged about 50% and at the same time they are raised upwards to the crutch. The experiments of Masters and Johnson demonstrate that orgasm and ejaculation follow at once upon this raising of the testicles. In the phase of orgasm the urethra tightens very considerably, so that the seminal fluid is ejaculated from the penis with increased force. Dependent on the intensity of the orgasm this contraction can last several seconds.

The last stage of the sexual reactions is divisible as far as the man is concerned into two levels. Immediately after orgasm there is a quick slackening of the penis, which is now only

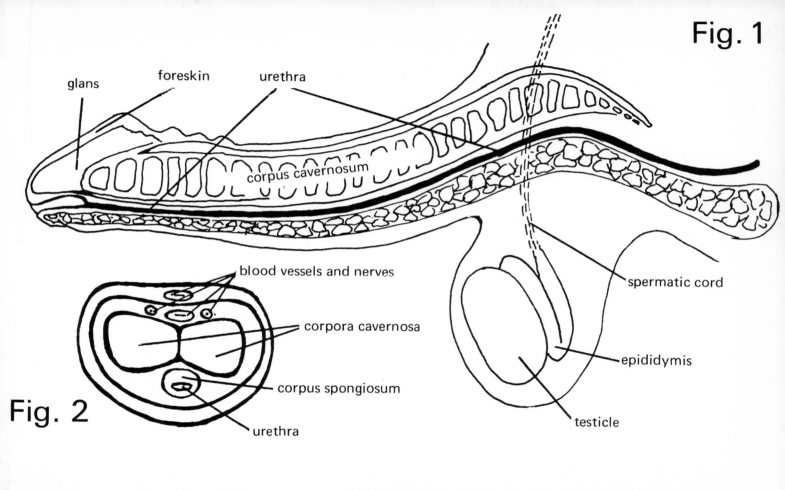

Fig. 1

glans   foreskin   urethra

corpus cavernosum

spermatic cord

epididymis

testicle

Fig. 2

blood vessels and nerves

corpora cavernosa

corpus spongiosum

urethra

twice the normal size. The second stage, where the penis regains its normal size, lasts somewhat longer; the man is now normally unable to have another erection immediately afterwards or any intercourse for the moment, a fact which is peculiar to him. Straight after the orgasm the man has a so-called "refractory" period which means that he, unlike the woman, is unable usually to react to any further sexual stimuli. The reason for this is not quite clear but it means in practice that the man must wait for some minutes, or even up to half an hour, before he is able to react to further stimuli with an erection and thus have intercourse again. The length of this period varies from one occasion to the next and it is very exceptional if a man can have further sex directly after orgasm and ejaculation.

It is worth mentioning that the glans penis or the whole penis, too, may be exceedingly sensitive to touch immediately after the orgasm. If this is the case than any further stimulation by the woman will bring no renewal of excitement. On the contrary, touching the penis can be so painful that it deprives the man of any further inclination for sex.
The man's sexual capacity will often depend on how long he can maintain his erection without reaching the orgasm. This can present a problem for many men but it is a problem which can almost always be solved. The glans penis of some men is so sensitive that even a light touch can produce an orgasm. This is called premature ejaculation and can be treated in various ways. There are various ointments having a local anaesthetic effect and these can reduce the sensitivity of the penis. There are also exercises available which are known to every doctor and specialist in sexual matters.

The thing to notice about these problems concerning virility, and it applies to most other sex difficulties of similar nature, is that they are by no means as insuperable as the people who suffer from them seem to think. Many men jib at the idea of asking their doctor for advice because they feel it is not a "manly" thing to do or to admit having any problem connected with impotence. Most men have doubted their virility at some time or other and most of this questioning, together with the problems connected with it, could be cleared away if only people would seek qualified help. Finally, an erection which is strong and enduring is not a prerequisite for the sexual satisfaction of the woman. On the contrary, for many women — perhaps for most of them — a finger or the tongue is a surer method of obtaining intense satisfaction than the lengthiest and most virile intercourse.

The Female Sex Organs

The parts of the female sex organs having erotic functions during intercourse are the vagina, the clitoris, the outer and inner lips and finally the breasts. Additional parts of the sex organs are the uterus, two ovaries and Fallopian tubes.

The ovaries play no direct part in the woman's sex life. They are, however, vitally important (but only indirectly) since the chief female sex hormone, oestrogen, is produced for the most part by these organs. Whether a woman is to lead a normal and satisfying sex life depends on the production of this hormone, but we shall not discuss them in greater detail since they have no direct influence upon erotic activity. This goes for the uterus too in some degree, but only up to a certain point since this organ shows a series of typical reactions during sexual excitement. In the first phase the uterus raises itself up a little. It is not known exactly whether the reason for this is that the ligaments holding the uterus swell up as a result of increased blood-supply and therefore become a little shorter or whether it has a totally different cause. During excitement the most characteristic feature in the physical reactions is that the organs in question are subjected to a violent increase in amount of blood from the rest of the body. This applies to the man when penis and testicles swell up and to the woman also, in whom the reaction can be yet more obvious than it is in the man.

In the plateau-phase, if sexual excitement is increasing, the uterus is lifted from the narrower part of the pelvic girdle, in which it normally lies, and held in the larger girdle until sexual stimulation has gone. In some women the uterus increases in size, especially in women who have been pregnant one or more times. This increase can be as much as 50% above the normal just before orgasm. During the latter the uterus contracts by means of the powerful muscles of the uterine walls and this is done in a way reminiscent of mild birth pangs.

This uterine contraction is not accompanied by pains but on the contrary contributes very considerably to an increase of intensity. The measurements carried out by Masters and Johnson of this process in the uterus demonstrated clearly that the physiological intensity of an orgasm could be measured in this way. The stronger the contractions had been the more intense the orgasm in the subjective opinion of the woman. Immediately after the orgasm, in the relaxation phase, a second reaction takes place in the uterus, during which the cervix widens so that it "yawns" towards the vagina where the semen is, under optimum conditions, collected after intercourse. This widening of the opening lasts about half an hour and it is presumed that the purpose of this is to facilitate passage of the sperms from the

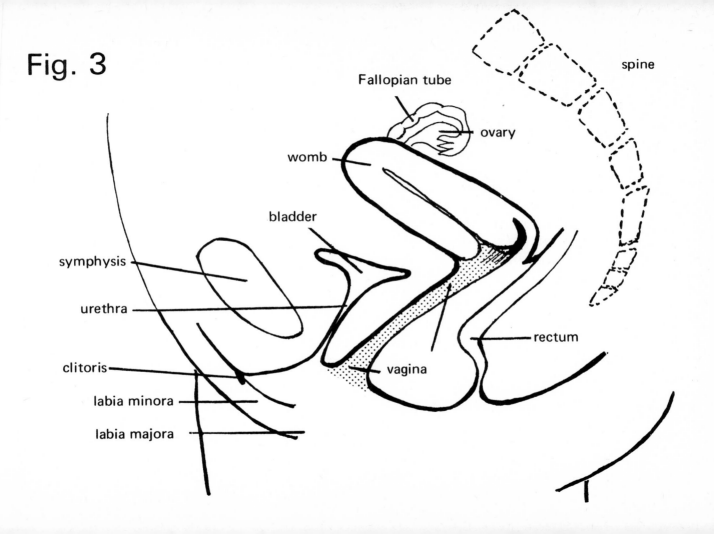

Fig. 3

spine

Fallopian tube

ovary

womb

bladder

symphysis

urethra

clitoris

labia minora

labia majora

vagina

rectum

vagina to the uterus so that fertilization can take place if necessary. At the same time the uterus descends again into the smaller pelvic region, so that the cervical area renews contact with the inner part of the vagina; a reaction which should improve the chances of fertilization.

It must be stated that the reactions just mentioned are not needed for orgasm. A woman can very easily experience sexual satisfaction without any strong reaction in the uterus. There are innumerable women leading a perfectly satisfactory sex life after the uterus has been removed by surgery. So the fact that the uterus is there and that it reacts in the manner described does not mean it is necessary for a satisfactory sex life as far as the woman is concerned: one can only state that the uterus, *if* it is there, displays these reactions which are probably all meant to increase the chances of fertilization.

The breasts are usually characterized as so-called secondary sex organs; which means that they have features in common with both sexes though without direct connection with sex life and reproduction. In both men and women, for instance, the breasts can react to sex stimuli but only in women are the reactions immediately observable.

In almost all women and in some men the nipples show a distinct erection at the beginning of stimulation. As far as most men are concerned the visible reactions to stimuli stop in the breasts at this point whereas women's breasts go through a series of reactions which follow a relatively fixed pattern. After the nipples have reacted initially one can often see a delicate pattern of veins on the frontal and lower surfaces of the breasts, which increase in size while the pigmented areas around the nipples swell up. In the plateau-phase the latter becomes still more erect, the breast grows bigger and the areola (the area round the nipple) become wider. During the orgasm itself a change in the woman's breasts cannot normally be observed, most of the signs of excitement tending to fade very quickly as a rule — sometimes they last only a few seconds — when the woman has reached the orgasm. This applies especially to the erection of the nipples and to the swelling of the areola, while the breast is returning somewhat more slowly to its normal size.

The breasts are very receptive to sexual stimuli, especially in women. With an even and rhythmical stroking of the breasts and especially of the nipples and the area around them the man can significantly increase the woman's excitement. Some women are enabled to reach orgasm only after such stimulation and among some it can be the cause of guilty feelings in certain circumstances, as for instance if they experience sexual satisfaction when breast-feeding. Feelings of guilt such as these are perfectly absurd since what is happening here is an absolutely natural reaction to a powerful sexual stimulus. No woman feels guilty because she is being sexually excited or because she has an orgasm if the man with whom she is living kisses her nipples or sucks them. If she feels the same lust whilst breast-feeding this is not a sign of incestuous connection with the child but only a perfectly natural physiological reaction, the purpose of which from nature's point of view is to induce the woman to accept her progeny and look after it. What applies here, as in all other cases, is that nature always takes her precautions with no regard for morals; and it is the morality which is wrong — not nature — if human philosophy regards natural reactions as if they are "indecent". For most men the breasts are not so sensitive to sex stimuli as those of women are — in fact far less so — but whether this is a reaction determined by sex is not clear, though certain scientific data would appear to show that this is not the case. It is known, for example, from enquiries into homosexual sex habits that the breasts are often capable of strong sexual excitement. This indicates a reaction due to a sexual habit only, which by continual stimulation can be altered to become intense excitement.

The Vagina

For the majority of men used to Western ideas and culture the vagina (see page 123) is probably the most important of the female sex organs both from the point of view of reproduction and love-making. There can hardly be any doubt about the former, since it is the vagina which receives the semen from the penis and thus makes a pregnancy possible. But the second supposition — that the vagina is also the most important organ with regard to intercourse — is hardly correct: many women would contest the assumption, and rightly.

The vagina is really a cavity in its normal, unstimulated state; that is, its walls in the absence of sexual excitement lie together or very nearly so, which means that it is not always right to think of it as directly accessible, as an ever-open tube.

In the unstimulated state the width of this tube varies from 1 to 2 centimetres, while its length can vary from 7 to 8 centimetres. The walls consist of very elastic muscular tissue lined with thick mucous membrane. One third of the "cover" of the vagina lies right at the back and is filled by the uterine orifice (opening) of the cervix or neck of the uterus. At the back the vagina ends like a cul-de-sac, the posterior wall of which likewise consists of very elastic muscular tissue.

The first signs of very strong sexual excitement are to be found in the vagina, the walls or mucous membranes of which secrete a viscous liquid as the very first reaction and this "oils" the whole organ so that the penis can easily enter. This first "dampness-reaction" occurs in most women within 30 seconds of any stimulation; and this does not have to be necessarily a physical one to start it going. Just as effective is a purely mental stimulus like erotic thoughts or the reading of pornography; and during this phase of excitement there is an increase in the diameter and length of the vagina, which according to Masters and Johnson is 5 to 6.5 centimetres for the former (towards the end of the phase) and about 10 centimetres for the latter. These measurements tell us nothing, however, about the maximum width of the vagina. To picture this one must think of the vaginal expansion during birth, when a child must pass along through the uterine orifice and thence through this organ. Here the dilation is many times the normal and without exception much larger than the increased width any penis can cause.

There is a further widening in the plateau-stage, as it grows longer and the diameter of the back two thirds also increases. The third nearest the outside changes shape but in this case the vaginal walls become thicker, with the result that the inner vaginal cavity is more or less closed, due to a strong increase in the amount of blood in the pelvis during excitement. This extra blood-supply is concentrated on the vagina and thus especially upon that third of the vagina which lies nearest the outside.

Masters and Johnson ascertained that this phenomenon appeared in all the women who took part in their experiments regarding the sexual reactions. They called this narrowing of this part of the vagina the "orgiastic platform" because it shows the strongest reactions during actual intercourse. The formation of this "platform" during coition indicates that the outer part of the vagina becomes smaller when the orgasm approaches, which entails increased pressure on the penis by the vaginal walls, and therefore further sexual stimulation of the man when the woman nears the crisis.

During the woman's orgasm a series of spasms are produced by the muscles of the vaginal walls, the contractions beginning in the orgiastic platform at the outer end of the vagina and occurring at intervals of 0.8 seconds. They may be repeated from 5 to 12 times and usually the first spasms are the strongest. After the initial three to five spasms the intervals become longer and the contractions weaker. These convulsive movements both in the platform and in the uterine walls give some idea of the intensity of the individual orgasm. If the spasms have been frequent and strong then the woman has experienced a very intense orgasm but if the movements were not so strong then neither was the crisis. A "normal orgasm" will probably comprise about 5 to 8 spasms.

These vaginal reactions are independent of the will and the woman is usually unable to distinguish the individual spasms in the orgiastic platform from each other; but it is not unusual for a woman to be able to produce after orgasm a number of contractions herself, by using the vaginal musculature. These can be consciously produced but the reaction itself is only partly subject to the will.

After the orgasm the platform in the vagina soon returns to normal and simultaneously the vaginal walls regain their usual size. The time taken varies with the intensity of the individual orgasm. If the woman reaches the plateau-stage without the satisfaction of orgasm then sexual excitement before orgasm lasted rather long. If such excitement was protracted and left unsatisfied by orgasm it can be several hours before the vagina returns to normal.

The Labia (Lips) of the Vulva

These cover and protect the vaginal orifice under normal circumstances and this applies especially to the outer lips which, if anatomically normal, cover the orifice, the inner lips and the clitoris. During parturition (birth) the outer lips can become scarred and thus lose their elasticity together with their ability to cover the vaginal orifice.

Reactions are also to be seen in the outer lips when a woman is sexually excited, and they are of two sorts, one being typical of women who are mothers and the other characteristic of those who have never given birth. One can generally say that the reactions in the outer lips are brought on by strong blood-supply during excitement, with results facilitating penis insertion by the lips becoming a little flatter and exposing the orifice. If the lips have been damaged during birth then the distinction between open and closed lips is not so marked.

They become larger in diameter but stay closed in the middle. In the plateau-phase the increased blood-supply to the outer lips continues and they can become very large, especially in women who have given birth. Orgasm itself produces no visible reactions in the lips, while in the stage of relaxation the blood ebbs relatively quickly unless the woman suffered injuries in giving birth. If she is troubled by broken blood-vessels in the lips then it lasts somewhat longer before all traces of sexual excitement have gone.

The parts of the female sex organs protected by the outer lips have the greatest sensitivity to stimuli — we mean of course the inner lips and the clitoris. The former are a double fold of skin lying on both sides of the vaginal orifice and which at the symphysis pubis lie over each other to form a foreskin over the clitoris. They are rich in nerves and are almost as receptive to sexual stimuli (e.g. touch) as is the clitoris. The most typical reaction of the inner lips appears in the first stage of the sexual cycle. A thickening of the two folds of skin now takes place, resulting in a stretching outwards away from the vaginal orifice and in the formation of a small duct which increases the length of the vagina by about 1 centimetre. Thus the inner lips during intercourse are in effect the first short piece of the vagina and are therefore exposed to powerful stimulation from the movements of the penis. It is not uncommon for this to be in fact the strongest stimulation, as far as the woman is concerned, during the whole intercourse; and since the inner lips also cover the clitoris with a thin foreskin the pulling movements exercised upon them by the penis acts at the same time like an indirect stimulus upon the clitoris because it spreads upwards — and thus causes a rubbing of the foreskin against the upper side of the clitoris. This indirect stimulation certainly has very considerable importance in the sexual satisfaction of the woman, and since in most positions this is the only possible way of stimulating the clitoris its significance is all the greater.

The inner lips undergo a number of changes in colour during the plateau-phase. According to Masters and Johnson, whose observations are based inter alia on photography, the colour shifts from its normal bright red to a deeper shade of burgundy-red, which according to both these workers means that the woman reaches the orgasm if the sex stimuli are continued. In the orgasm-phase one can detect special reactions in the inner lips but afterwards they change again, within a few seconds, from the dark-red to the normal bright colour.

The Clitoris

This is the organ having the largest share in the work of sexual reaction and female satisfaction. Anatomically it closely resembles the penis. It consists of two bodies which, like the corpora cavernosa in the penis are filled with cavities, and which can produce a stiffening of the organ similar to that of the penis when sexually excited and blood-filled.

Like the penis the clitoris is richly supplied with nerves and this fact makes it the most sensitive of the female sexual organs.

Normally the clitoris is fully covered by the fold of skin which the inner lips form over it. Its size can vary considerably but is usually about 2 to 5 centimetres. As in the case of the penis it has a body and head and is similarly connected to the pelvis by a tissue of tendons and muscular fibres.

Whenever a man is sexually excited the first certain sign is erection, starting within seconds and lasting — perhaps with interruptions — until the man has sexual satisfaction; but the stimulation itself, however, must be uninterrupted. In the woman the first sign of excitement, and the surest, is an increase in vaginal moisture; a reaction which appears so quickly that it can be compared with penis erection, but it is only later that evidence of sexual excitement is revealed in the clitoris itself. The latter organ shows its reaction by a gentle swelling of the glans of the clitoris i.e. the very sensitive part on its head. However, this reaction does not occur in all women and even when it is there it is often so small a reaction that it cannot be observed by the naked eye. At the same time there is a lengthening and thickening of the clitoris-body itself during this phase, but here again it is often a reaction limited in extent and difficult to see or feel. If the woman's excitement rises to the plateau-phase there is a lasting clitoris reaction of great practical significance for both partners. The whole clitoris withdraws, so that it is no longer capable of being stimulated in its customary position. The cause of this reaction is not clear but it is not improbable that it is a form of protection against a too strong effect upon the extremely sensitive clitoris-head. This area, known as the glans clitoridis, has so many nerves that a protracted stimulus upon it can have a completely different effect than the one intended. Instead of being an erotic stimulus it may irritate the sensitive surface of the clitoris, especially if the stimulation lasts too long or if it is manual and not gentle enough. This of course, instead of increasing desire in the woman, has just the opposite effect. This reaction was not universally known before Masters and Johnson discovered it in their labaratory investigations. If a man is unaware of the fact and fails to grasp its nature he is often confused by it and becomes uncertain. It means in practice that while the man is stimulating the clitoris manually it may suddenly become impossible to find and by groping around to do so he makes the woman's excitement subside in most cases; but this does not exclude the possibility of a further stimulation later. Both the inner lips and the whole area around the customary position of the clitoris are exceedingly receptive to sexual stimuli; even the lightest pressure or superficial stroking causes indirect stimulation of the clitoris, which for the woman is much more exciting than a useless search or attempt to regain direct touch with the organ.

Since the clitoris remains for the rest of the sexual cycle in its withdrawn position until the woman has had her orgasm it was not possible hitherto to establish whether during orgasm it showed any reaction itself. At any rate Masters and Johnson have ascertained that it lasts only 10 to 15 seconds, reckoning from the start of orgasm, before the clitoris is back in its normal position; and if the glans or the clitoris-shaft itself has been in a swollen state then this swelling ebbs away somewhat more slowly.

The Female Orgasm

The concept of sex nowadays is an extremely confused phenomenon, and is used so widely that when one finally comes to the point it often works as an anti-climax. It could seem as if its practical possibilities of development would never equal the number of raised hands, well-intended advice and pretended extravagances. This is at once both more or less inevitable as well as unfair. Inevitable, because people usually talk too much about it and are not active enough in the matter; and because the many taboos, mysteries and demons which have influenced the sex life of the western world can only harm the actual facts, which for good reasons have to compete with the sexual knowledge and ability of quite ordinary people.

It is also unfair because this host of taboos and prejudices rob an endless number of people of the chance of individual enjoyment and personal development in its many and varied ways.

One of the aspects of sexual life, which for generations has been a source of dispute, whether of severely scientific nature or of popular illustrated-magazine type, is the question of whether, when and above all how a woman obtains sexual satisfaction.

Be that as it may, there are innumerable women for whom this is a burning problem. Just as there are many men who have to contend with problems concerning impotence there are also many women who suffer from what is popularly — and wrongly-called frigidity. The reasons for these problems are probably just as numerous and varied as are their victims, since they can all be due to anatomical or physiological defects; or to psychological complications. It is not unlikely that this last is the commonest category but the possibility is also very considerable that they arise from a combination of two or three factors.

Regardless of the cause the chances of a solution are high if one consults a doctor or sexologist, since the reason is often misunderstanding or ignorance, and the resulting miseries can be done away with for ever by a simple conversation or two. And if this should not be the case both psychology and medicine have at their disposal today a number of methods of treatment applicable when the problem is one within the realm of sex.

What is much more absurd is that both the expert and the layman can have long and heated discussions about which of the two hypothetical forms of orgasm is the correct one for the woman. This is necessarily a storm in a teacup if one considers the matter objectively, because orgasm is by definition sexual satisfaction; and what else can one demand of sexual intercourse?

If we consider this discussion in a detached fashion it seems unfortunately rather more harmful than absurd, since in many women it could cause doubt and sexual frustration in place of their genuine conviction that their sex lives were perfectly satisfying and normal. For just suppose there was a "false" orgasm! It is hardly any consolation to them to share both doubt and frustration with those who take part so enthusiastically in the debate.

With regard to the possible "victims" of this controversy of clitoris versus vaginal orgasm it would probably be as well to mention what the sexologists know about human sexual reactions.

Excitement can be caused and maintained in a variety of ways. Kinsey lists the following methods in his famous book on the woman's sex life: — masturbation, nocturnal sex-dreams, "petting", sexual intercourse, homosexual relationships, sexual phantasies. Since the work of Masters and Johnson was published a further method might be added to this list — that of artificial intercourse: for this method Masters and Johnson built an electrically powered penis so that the female members of the team engaged in the research could practise artificial coition. This penis was manufactured from a material possessing the same brittleness as mirror-glass and equipped with a miniature camera using colour-film so that the reactions in the vagina during intercourse could be studied.

One of the chief aims of this research by Masters and Johnson was to find out whether the body reacted in different ways to different sexual stimuli. Put in another way this means that they tried to ascertain whether a person has the same sexual excitement and satisfaction regardless of the nature of the stimulus. In order to obtain a norm for their comparisons they employed a series of scientifically recognized methods of measurement in more than

7,500 sexually complete reaction-cycles in women alone.

If we stress sexually complete reaction-cycles we do so to make it clear that these are cycles which are sexually complete, from the first excitement to a final satisfaction by one or more orgasms. In these experiments various means of stimulation were applied: there was heterosexual intercourse, masturbation and artificial copulation. In all the cases it was possible to assert that the reactions measured were identical, no matter what the nature of the sexual stimulus. But this must be qualified by the fact that there was a tendency to a more powerful orgasm if the stimulus was masturbation.

One can therefore state that the scientific experiments connected with sexual reactions which have so far been carried out have concluded that the woman's orgasm — as far as a purely physiological point of view is concerned — is of the same nature and has the same satisfaction irrespective of the type of stimulation.

In order to establish a better basis for their conclusions Masters and Johnson asked their female collaborators to give a subjective description of their experiences resulting from the different stimuli involved. The general consensus of opinion was that orgasm was more intense after masturbation than after intercourse; i.e., a manually induced orgasm was more satisfying from the point of view of a purely personal and psychological assessment.

Amongst all these physiological facts and details connected with them there is the fact that most women can obtain the greatest satisfaction from a manually induced orgasm if this is carried out by an erotically attractive partner with whom she shares emotional ties. This is probably true, but it does not mean that there are women who can be sexually satisfied *only* by manual manipulation, any more than women finding sexual happiness *solely* by intercourse. And finally there is also the possibility that very many women experience the highest enjoyment from a combination of both methods.

Masters and Johnson also established that many women are capable of several orgasms during a single act of sexual intercourse. In fact this means a whole series of orgasms with one leading directly into the next; or there can be several clearly distinguishable orgasms with intervals of seconds or minutes in between. From the woman's point of view this must presumably be ideal intercourse. It is most important that both the woman and her partner have the necessary knowledge and really want to obtain the utmost pleasure, which in practice means effective, direct stimulation of the clitoris in order to produce the first very strong orgasm. After that the woman will probably try to obtain deep satisfaction from a fully completed act of intercourse with her partner; or she may prefer to try this straight away instead.

Sex and Pregnancy

This book deals mainly with the erotic side of sexual life, chief emphasis being laid upon the significance of physiological knowledge and varied methods when a sexually happy life is the aim. But full enjoyment requires that both man and woman can enjoy it, in fact, with complete freedom from fear of undesired results, such as a pregnancy — there must be relaxation, not tension.

The fear of an unwanted pregnancy can have a totally paralysing effect as far as woman's sexual reactions are concerned; and even if the man in many cases does not experience this anxiety so keenly as the woman, nervousness and inhibitions will very often have a bad effect upon their sexual experiences. This is a problem which can be solved in a variety of ways, the most primitive of which — but also unfortunately the commonest — is coitus interruptus i.e. withdrawal before ejaculation. The method is very simple, consisting merely in the fact that the man removes his penis from the vagina before his orgasm, so that the semen does not reach the uterus. But as a means of contraception it is so unsafe that it really cannot be called a contraceptive method at all. Even if the man can control his ejaculation so well that he withdraws before orgasm it is certainly no guarantee that no sperms are left behind in the vagina. On the front part of the penis just inside the opening of the urethra there are several glands — the Cowper glands. A little while before orgasm these bodies secrete a few drops of liquid which often contain living sperms, which means that the woman can conceive *even if the man's orgasm takes place outside the vagina.* Whether the woman knows this or not she will often distrust the man's self-control and the whole procedure, for reasons easy to understand. As a result she is tense all the time and is very alert to the slightest sign that the male orgasm is approaching; which means that the man will be adversely effected, so that intercourse usually fails entirely.

Undoubtedly many people, and most likely the majority, know this situation. If both partners are sexually inexperienced it is a situation which can cause much more damage than is tolerable; if a pregnancy has been avoided or not, it makes no difference — this still applies. Youths and young men in our society are almost always very uncertain of themselves and their sexual capacities, and this uncertainty is quite naturally at its most extensive until one has acquired a certain practical experience. If the "first time" is an experience attended by the sort of thing just mentioned then this can have long-term effects which are very difficult to overcome. As far as the girl is concerned such an experience is inevitably followed by anxieties for days, or even for a month, until her next period comes; after which she breathes a sigh of relief and promises herself that in future she will never have anything to do with sex again.

A much more satisfactory solution for both partners would undoubtedly be mutual petting and onanism (masturbation) until they master the situation with a proper supply of contraceptives. It is therefore advisable to mention the commonest methods of birth-control; readers who need more detailed information can find it in the many books on this subject which have appeared in the last few years, or they can ask a doctor — perhaps the best thing to do.

There are three classes of contraceptives viz.: — those based on biological, those on chemical principles and finally those having mechanical principles.

The first category is represented by the Pill, which during recent years has found world-wide acceptance and is probably the safest and most practical method we possess today. It consists of concentrations of certain hormones natural to the human body. There are several systems using various harmones, but most of them (and probably the most suitable ones) are based on substances derived from the progesterone hormone, which hinders ovulation and therefore pregnancy; that is, any further one.

The contraceptive pill can be obtained on prescription, in packages large enough to last a month, and with exact instructions concerning the way in which they must be taken. Many doctors prescribe enough to last up to six months. Every day for 20 days consecutively one pill must be taken. Menstruation then takes place and there is an interval of 5 to 7 days before starting again with the pills. The procedure can vary somewhat, depending on the brand of pill, so it is necessary to follow medical instructions exactly, in every case. It should be stressed that as long as one does this the pill is completely reliable; but the possibility of a pregnancy is *increased* if one suddenly stops taking them half-way through a period. In some cases, therefore, this method may actually cause a pregnancy.

Much has been said and written about the side-effects of the Pill. As far as concerns those substances manufactured from the male sex hormone called testosterone it is true that there are some cases of adverse side-effects, especially if the woman concerned has been taking the pill for a long time. Such side-effects may be shown for instance by an increase in facial hair or a deepening of the voice; or other and similar influences upon the secondary sexual organs, but they disappeared again when the woman recommenced her practice of taking female sex hormone. The side-effects most commonly discussed e.g. sickness, or some influence upon the woman's sexual needs, are usually only a passing phenomenon which vanish after 1 to 2 months. And as one can justifiably assume at the same time that the pill, besides acting as a contraceptive, has other and positive influences then no woman should be dissuaded from taking them because of these side-effects.

One is partly justified in stating that the *safe days* are a biological means of contraception, but not always to be recommended, in fact not at all. It is a method which is presumably no more useful than coitus interruptus and is based on the supposition that ovulation occurs more or less exactly on the fourteenth day after menstruation, so that each period has certain safe days. But since in the first place one cannot be quite certain that ovulation will occur with such extreme regularity (it may, for example, be delayed by anxiety about pregnancy) and in the second place one can never be quite sure how long a sperm can live in the uterus, then it is not exaggerated if we say that this method is not one based on rational, scientific principles. But what can be said in its favour is that it is the only one permitted by the Catholic Church.

The two best known mechanical methods are the pessary and the condom (sheath). The pessary is a small cup made of soft rubber but with a firm rim. It is placed in the vagina just in front of the opening of the uterus, where it prevents the penetration of sperms into that organ. A paste is usually put on it and this not only shuts off the entrance more completely but also kills the sperms. But if the pessary is to function efficiently the measurements must be taken by a doctor who at the time may also supply detailed instructions about its insertion. It is put in before intercourse begins and must not be removed until 6 or 8 hours afterwards. The method is an extremely reliable one if the medical instructions are properly followed, but it should be borne in mind that in the case of a fairly young woman who is measured for a pessary the size of it should be checked at least once a year. After a birth, too, or following an abdominal operation, it should always be checked for correct size.

The condom is somewhat less safe but on the other hand easier to buy as it does not require any medical help. They are available in all chemists and barbers' shops etc.

For men who have problems of premature ejaculation the sheath is the best answer because it reduces the sensitivity of the glans penis to a certain degree; and has the further advantage of preventing venereal diseases to some extent if it is the only contraceptive being used.

The various types of coils in use are among the oldest contraceptives known, the principle of it having been used for at least 4000 years. Just as we employ the intra-uterine ring today, we know from a description that semen was used by nomads in ancient Mesopotamia in the same way, when they wanted to limit the number of their young camels in years of drought and bad pastures. Nowadays it is a small plastic or nylon device which is put into the uterus by a doctor. Actually it is placed in the neck of the uterus and thus prevents the passage of sperms. How it functions is not known with absolute certainty. The neck of the uterus is not closed, since the ring does not hinder the menstrual flow through the neck of this organ. There is no complete unanimity about the reliability of this method, since the ring itself is very small and it *could* slip out without the woman being aware of the fact herself and thus being completely exposed to the chance of pregnancy. A second disadvantage is that for purely anatomical reasons not all women can use it. But in its favour is the fact that it is extremely practical: once inserted it is there for good, which means in effect a period of several years in many cases. It works by itself and the woman has no bother with pessaries and pills.

Apart from the contraceptive methods mentioned here there are several chemical preparations available for purchase, chiefly pastes and ointments which are lethal to sperms.

Many of these products can be had without prescription but before using them it is always best to consult a doctor. None of them has the same degree of safety as is offered by the Pill, pessary and condom, but some can be employed with advantage in addition to the pessary, etc.